# TRUCKS IN BRITAIN

# DRAWBAR OUTFITS

**FRONT COVER PHOTOGRAPH:**
1977 Leyland Buffalo fitted with the fixed-head 500 diesel engine, pictured in the livery of Bedfordshire-based operator R. Lockey.

First published in 1992 by
**Roundoak Publishing,**
**Nynehead,**
**Wellington,**
**Somerset,**
**England, TA21 0BX.**

ISBN 1-871565-15-4

**REAR COVER PHOTOGRAPHS:**

**TOP:**
1962 S21 cabbed Foden 8-wheeler & trailer of Knowles Transport, Wimblington — photographed when new in the haulier's yard.

**BOTTOM:**
1990 Iveco Ford Cargo close-coupled outfit from Eddie Stobart's large Carlisle-based fleet.

Published by Roundoak Publishing.

Design and typesetting by
**Haight Ashbury Design,**
**Stoke Sub Hamdon, Somerset.**

Printed in Great Britain by
**The Mathews Wright Press,**
**Chard, Somerset.**

# ACKNOWLEDGEMENTS

The author greatly appreciates the assistance he has received in the compilation of this book, especially from those who supplied pictures including Jack Butterworth, Michael Cramp, Arthur Ingram, Roger Kenney, Tony Knowles, Howard Nunnick, Bill Packham, John Richardson and Jim Taylor.

# TRUCKS IN BRITAIN

# DRAWBAR OUTFITS

## Peter Davies

ROUNDOAK PUBLISHING

# INTRODUCTION

Drawbar outfits come in different forms but for the purpose of this book we can define the subject as the 'lorry and trailer' used for normal every day haulage. At the same time a few examples of other types such as those used in dock haulage, heavy haulage and showman's transport have been included. Specialised trailers carrying permanently mounted plant and equipment are not covered to any great degree, the main emphasis being on load carrying vehicles.

The drawbar trailer has been around for a long time and shares many of its characteristics with the old fashioned horse-drawn wagons of the mid nineteenth century. In principle those rudimentary wooden wagons were trailers although it could be argued that with a horse hitched between the shafts they formed artics. Indeed some horse-drawn wagons were adapted for use behind motor vehicles in the early days. Earlier still, steam traction engines were used in conjunction with drawbar trailers. So the trailer has certainly been around longer than the motor lorry.

By and large British drawbar combinations consist of a lorry with one trailer. While a lorry can only be legally loaded to its design limit, usually governed by spring and tyre capacities, it can cope with more load both in mass and volume if hauled in traction. Drawbar trailers are particularly effective where light, bulky goods are carried such as straw bales, furniture, glass bottles or empty oil drums.

The demand for any particular type of truck is greatly influenced by legislation. It is nearly always legislative change which spawns new development rather than vice versa even if new inventions or influence from other countries bring some force to bear on those who draft the law. In one way or another the use of drawbar trailers in Britain has always been discriminated against through speed and weight restrictions. For example in 1953 when the 20 mph limit for lorries over three tons unladen was raised to 30, drawbar outfits were still restricted to 20. Only during the past decade have drawbar outfit speed limits been aligned with solo vehicles and artics. When the maximum legal gross weight was raised to 38 tons for artics in 1983, drawbar outfits once again were held back to 32 tons. A minor increase to 35 tonnes is planned from January 1993.

British law has never permitted the use of drawbar trailers behind artics. Such 'double' outfits have proved perfectly safe and efficient in several countries and indeed were tried in Britain in the late Sixties and early Seventies under special dispensation. However their use is still illegal under British legislation. Also the pulling of more than one trailer is illegal except in the case of showman's vehicles and ballast tractors used around the docks. Before the advent of power-assisted trailer brakes which operated simultaneously when the driver applied the normal lorry brakes all trailer outfits in the UK had to carry a second man or 'statutory attendant'. This law was rescinded as recently as 1970. The attendant was originally employed to work the massive pull-on handbrake lever situated in front of the passenger seat. This was mechanically linked by rods and cables to the rearmost axle of the drawbar trailer. Some vehicles had special footrests against which the attendant could brace himself to get maximum leverage.

Prior to about 1960 the typical four wheel drawbar trailer was of very simple construction. It was coupled to a hook on the lorry or through a lift-out pin to a 'jaw' mounted on the rearmost crossmember of the lorry chassis. Sometimes the jaw was spring loaded to damp out shock loadings but many were rigidly mounted with a crude brace on to each sidemember to take the strain. Cross chains were usually slung from hooks between lorry and trailer as an additional safeguard in case the trailer pin became displaced or sheared.

Brake connections consisted of a simple cable or, in the case of those with power-assisted brakes, a detachable vacuum or air line. An electrical cable was also provided to feed the trailer rear lights. If the trailer braking robbed too much vacuum or air from the lorry's own system it was not unknown for drivers to blank off the trailer supply altogether whilst leaving the hoses connected for appearance sake.

Since legislation was tightened in the Sixties trailers have far more sophisticated drawbar couplings and braking systems, the latter employing three line (service auxiliary and emergency) supplies and modern trailers are of course braked on all wheels.

Lorries built specifically for trailer use are usually specified with additional compressed air capacity as well as having higher powered engines and heavy duty multi-speed transmissions similar to artic tractor units. Years ago they tended to have lower overall gearing when

19th century farm cart — forerunner of the modern drawbar trailer.

intended for use at full train weight especially as they were limited to 20 mph. The war-time Maudslay Mogul, a popular trailer model, carried a brass plate on the dashboard advising drivers not to use top gear when drawing a trailer.

Sometimes vehicles which were only designed for solo use were seen drawing trailers — types such as those from Bedford, Ford and Commer. In most cases this was to achieve greater load volume rather than weight although some were loaded well over the limit especially during the Thirties and Forties.

Britain is not generally regarded as being drawbar minded, certainly not in the same way as Germany, Sweden, Switzerland and Italy. Nevertheless it has been the home of many reputed trailer manufacturers. Among the best known of these were R A Dyson of Liverpool, Cranes of Dereham, Taskers of Andover, Carrimore of Finchley and Eagle of Warwick. If anything the archetypal trailer of the early post war period was the 8-ton Dyson widely used by British Road Services. Normally they were mounted with flat bodywork 16ft long by 7ft 6in wide and were braked on the rear axle only. Most were fitted with mudguards on the rear wheels but sometimes front wheels were completely unguarded.

Many think of the late Forties and Fifties as the heyday of British haulage, being the period when BRS was fully operational. This was certainly an era when trailer outfits were very common on long distance work. Even then, long before the advent of maximum weight artics in 1964 an eight wheeler and trailer could gross 32 tons providing that it met with the Construction & Use Regulations on braking.

At that weight a machine such as an ERF or Atkinson with its 102-112 bhp Gardner 6LW was not adequately powered, bearing in mind too that there were hardly any main routes without steep hills in the pre motorway era. AECs, Leylands and Maudslays were the most common 'Max-cap' (maximum capacity) eight wheeler and trailer outfits having more powerful engines of 125-150 bhp.

The term 'drawbar outfit' is relatively modern. 'Trailer outfit' was more in general use until about 20 years ago. Drivers had their own terms, such as 'wagon and drag', 'lorry and dangler' or 'wagon and pup'. Traditionally a lorry would be known as a 'trailer model' if it was suitable for drawbar use. Typical examples were the Leyland Beaver and AEC Mandator. Now the term 'drawbar unit' tends to be favoured befitting the artic era.

A new breed of truck appeared in the early Eighties namely the centre bogie close-coupled outfit. This has become popular for long distance and Continental haulage. One could argue that it is not so much a drawbar outfit as an artic in that the trailer, supported on a centre-mounted bogie, is pivoted through a rigid 'A' frame to the coupling mounted well forward on the truck's chassis near to the rear axle. The difference being that no part of the trailer weight is imposed on the drawing vehicle. In principle it is a giant version of the trailer one might tow behind the family car. Such outfits have been common in Switzerland, Holland and certain other countries for some years.

'Drawbar-Semi' might aptly describe such a trailer but in the eyes of the law it is regarded as a normal drawbar and is therefore permitted to measure up to 18.35m overall length as opposed to 16.5m for an artic. The great benefit of the 'close-coupled' outfit is its added deck length and load volume. With short day cab, up to 15.65m of deck length is possible as compared with about 14m on normal drawbar outfits. With modern technology drawbars can be made to automatically adjust to prevent fouling of the lorry and trailer on steep ramps. Close-coupled outfits with normal four wheel trailers have also been developed using self-adjusting drawbars. Interesting designs have appeared like that from the German Ackerman Fruehauf concern. Also from Germany is the PAL system which provides progressive automatic adjustment up to 600mm.

When it comes to historical interest we tend to remember trailer outfits not by their trailers but by the lorries that pull them. This pictorial record of British trailer outfits therefore focuses on the lorries first and foremost and indeed, in many cases it is difficult to even identify the exact details of the trailers. It not only looks back almost to the beginning of motor transport but comes right up to the minute and in doing so serves as a unique historical round up on a relatively undocumented subject. Some makes have been given wider coverage than others because certain trucks were more popular for drawbar work whilst others were rarely seen with a trailer. British registered European trucks are also included for interest value as they form such a large part of our present day lorry population.

Close-coupled drawbar outfit from Ackerman Fruehauf.

AEC

This early Thirties photograph showing three AEC Mammoths clearly demonstrates one advantage of drawbar operation. Light, bulky goods such as these hops demand the maximum possible load area. The trailer outfit at the centre is carrying at least 60% more bulk than the 'solo' lorries.
*(Author's collection)*

A 1948 registered AEC Matador with Luton body and Dyson boxvan trailer from the well known fleet of Harrisons of Dewsbury. It features the open roof with tarpaulin cover once frequently seen on Yorkshire based vehicles, facilitating overhead loading. The cab appears to have been modernised probably by Holmalloy of Preston. *(A. Ingram)*

This 1937 Mammoth Minor outfit photographed during wartime captures the atmosphere of the period with its headlamp mask required during the 'blackout'. Note the single wheels on the third axle. The lorry grossed up to 16-tons solo and 22-tons with trailer. *(H. Nunnick collection)*

A Regal bus chassis forms the basis of this unusual outfit providing an ultra low loading height. It was one of a number operated on the transport of glass by Pilkington's of St. Helens.
*(Author)*

*(Below):* If one had to choose a picture which summed up the classic Fifties lorry and trailer outfit this would surely be it. Loaded to the 'gunnels' with woollen bales and bearing one of the most famous names in British haulage — Hansons of Huddersfield — this Mammoth Major Mk.III dates from 1956.
*(R Kenney collection)*

Typical of South Yorkshire haulage vehicles is this Mammoth Major MkIII six wheeled flat and 16ft Dyson drawbar trailer photographed at Henry Long's Manningham depot, Bradford in 1966. *(Author)*

A little more unusual in the drawbar line is this 1950 Duramin-cabbed short wheelbase Mammoth Major 3871 bulk sugar tanker coupled to a matching tipping trailer. The insulated tank bodies were specially designed for refined granulated sugar and were among the earliest specialised 'bulkers' to appear in the UK. Of Tate & Lyle's large bulker fleet only six were AECs, the remainder being of Foden manufacture. *(Author's collection)*

AECs had few rivals when it came to eight wheelers for trailer operation, the main competition coming from Leyland's famous Octopus. Both offered an extra margin of power compared with other 'eight leggers', most of which had the lower powered Gardner 6LW. This 1955 'tin front' Mk.III of Silver Roadways hauled goods for Tate & Lyle Ltd. *(Author's collection)*

British Road Services monopolised long distance traffic in the early Fifties and drawbar trailers were used widely both on general haulage and on parcels services. The most common trailer was probably the 16ft 8-ton Dyson of the type seen here coupled to a 1947 Matador Mk.II parcels van based in the London City area. The Matador was absorbed into BRS from Carter Paterson. *(Author's collection)*

Many hauliers in the Sixties experimented with standard semi trailers coupled to the lorry via a fifth wheel 'dolly'. It took the law some time to determine whether this arrangement was legal or not in that the 'dolly' was classed as a trailer in itself and therefore two trailers were being drawn. Test cases settled the argument in favour of allowing such outfits. This impressive 7-axled combination from Crow's of Gateshead is headed by a Mammoth Major with Ergomatic tilt cab. *(A. Ingram)*

This 1949 Mandator ran in the fleet of Samuel Williams based at Rainham, Essex. The trailer has narrow track axles with dual eight stud wheels instead of the more common ten stud singles. The outfit features a well balanced load of woollen bales. *(A. Ingram)*

Following the lifting of the 'second man' law on trailer outfits in 1970 there was an increase in popularity especially with four wheelers as they could legally operate up to 32 tons with a length limit of 59ft 1in. This gave more deck length than an artic and the driver, ironically, only needed a Class 3 HGV licence — the easiest class to obtain. These 1973 'Ergomatics', one a Mercury, the other a higher powered Mandator, are typical examples.
*(Author)/(Author's collection)*

ALBION

*(Top far left):* One of the oldest Albion drawbar pictures on record is this A10 chain-drive lorry coupled to a former horsedrawn wagon loaded with a heavy riveted steel vessel from John Jackson & Co who, like Albions, were based at Scotstoun, Glasgow. The photograph is believed to date from around 1912.
*(J. Butterworth collection)*

*(Top left):* Delivered just after the outbreak of World War II in 1939 this CX1S 6/7.5 ton lorry with its much older Dyson drawbar trailer was operated by the Canning Town Glass Works on the transport of glass bottles. Powered by an EN.236 4-cylinder diesel engine the CX1 was in production between 1936 and 1950.
*(J. Butterworth collection)*

*(Left):* Though not the most manoeuvrable of outfits whether in forward or reverse the Chinese Six and trailer was once a common sight on Britain's roads. For sheer perfection in this class of outfit, this 1939 CX27 of the Northern Despatch Motor Company, Darwen Bank Garage, could have few rivals. Adding to the period atmosphere are the granite paved roads and tramlines.
*(Author's collection)*

*(Above):* This 1950 Albion CX3 from the well known fleet of J. Lyons carries two old style demountable containers advertising Lyons' main products. Note the way in which the containers are roped on and the 'Danger' notice hanging from the drawbar warning other road users that there is a trailer following. *(A. Ingram)*

Another CX3, this time a 1946 model featuring insulated van bodywork on both the lorry and its Dyson trailer. The outfit appears in the brown and cream livery of J. Ward and Sons and was used to transport meat to and from Smithfield Market. *(A. Ingram)*

Less common as a trailer outfit is this 1955 Chieftain coupled to a relatively heavy 8-ton Dyson trailer. With its 75 bhp 4-cylinder diesel the Chieftain was hardly suitable for hauling heavy trailers except for shunting in unladen condition. This shot was taken in Rochdale where J. & T. Sharrocks were based.
*(R Kenney)*

Albion's CX7N rigid eight appeared in the late Thirties and resumed production after the Second World War in 1946. The post war version was virtually unchanged and continued in production until 1951. They were not frequently seen in drawbar form. This outfit, in the livery of The Barnsley Brewery Co, dates from 1947.
*(Author's collection)*

Hanson Haulage of Huddersfield were undoubtedly one of the best known trunk haulage operators running between South Yorkshire and London in the Fifties. This HD53 van pulls a tidily roped and sheeted Dyson trailer and the statutory 'second man' sometimes called the trailer mate leans nonchalantly from the window as they set out through north London on the first leg of their journey up the Great North Road.
(A. Ingram)

ATKINSON

*(Top, far left):* Dating from 1948 this Atkinson M1266 flat with 16ft 8-ton drawbar trailer is from the fleet of Road Services (Forth) Ltd. The substantial front shunting bar has an easily removable offside pin so that the bar can be hinged out to clear the starting handle. AEC pattern front hub rings pre date the full hub cap which was fitted to the later 'bow front' types.
*(A. Ingram)*

*(Top left):* In the Sixties the Port of Liverpool was noted for its old lorry and trailer outfits, George Davies being amongst the best known hauliers in the area. This four wheel Atkinson and trailer is an excellent example, crewed as usual by a driver and statutory attendant as required by law prior to 1970.
*(Author)*

*(Left):* Seven years newer than the Forth vehicle this 1955 L1266 coupled to a 20ft crane platform trailer has 11.00x20 front tyres giving additional load capacity to the front axle. The 'bow front' coachbuilt cab was standard equipment and full hub caps are featured on the front wheels which have a narrow offset to suit the large tyres. Aaron Henshall of Prescot, Lancs, hauled Triplex glass and were taken over by Holt Lane Transport also of Prescot.
*(Author)*

Fond memories will endure amongst enthusiasts of Holt Lane Transport's celebrated lorry and trailer fleet — probably the last large scale traditional operation of its kind in Britain. Holt Lane's fleet of Mk.I Atkinsons was based at Prescot near Liverpool and regularly hauled cable for the BICC. This 1967 model photographed at their premises in 1971 was typical of their superb outfits.
*(Author)*

Lancashire was particularly well endowed with lorry and trailer outfits. One of the best known hauliers from the area was Sutton & Sons (St. Helens) Ltd who operated this neatly loaded L1066 Chinese Six flat coupled to a 20ft 10-ton payload drawbar trailer shod on dual wheels all round.
*(R. Kenney)*

# AUSTIN

Austin was not a popular make for trailer use but for dock to market operation BRS Meat Haulage had a number of these 'Series III' tugs used in conjunction with four wheel independent trailers carrying insulated meat containers.
*(Author)*

# AWD

Following General Motors' decision to end production of Bedford trucks in 1986 AWD Ltd took over the Dunstable plant to continue building a range of civilian and military vehicles under the AWD name badge. Though similar in appearance to the former Bedford TL1630 'Techliner', this machine in drawbar form would be powered by the 265 bhp Cummins C-series turbo with Eaton 9-speed range change gearbox and Rockwell rear axle. Designated a TL17-27 it grossed 32 tonnes. AWD went into receivership in June 1992 after less than six years production.
*(Author's collection)*

BEDFORD

*(Top far left):* When it comes to impressive-looking loads this 1934 Bedford WT 3-tonner scores maximum points. Based at Moston, Manchester, the outfit made daily trips over the demanding A62 route across the Pennines to South Yorkshire. Sawdust suppliers Frederick Reeves operated the vehicle which was powered by the Bedford 64 bhp six-cylinder ohv petrol engine. *(Vauxhall Motors Ltd)*

*(Bottom far left):* Though in a similar weight class to Austin, Bedford trucks of the Fifties were occasionally seen hauling trailers, especially for applications such as this impressive 1960 car transporter loaded with nine Fiat '500' and '600' baby saloons. It was used in conjunction with Silver City Airways' cross-channel services by W. Gray & Sons of Folkestone and features a Burtonwood hydraulic loading ramp. *(Burtonwood Eng.)*

*(Top left):* Another slightly different form of car transporter is this Bedford TK with lightweight single bogie trailer. The nett load of five Land-Rovers would have been around 6.5 to 7 tons. *(Author)*

*(Bottom left):* Chadwick's of Halewood, Liverpool, were determined to make their 1972 Bedford KM work for its living. The '466' diesel must have been near its limit powering this outfit at 22 ton gtw. *(Author)*

In 1973 BRS Parcels Ltd Leicester Branch tried out a new concept of trunk vehicle in the form of this TK 1470 drawbar outfit. BRS Parcels, forerunner of today's Lynx Express Delivery Network, were at that time using large numbers of medium weight artics with automatic couplings on their trunk services, employing the 'changeover' system. This TK and trailer were of the skeletal type with Penco demountable modular van bodies. Swapping bodies was controlled by variable height air suspension.
*(Author)*

An example of weight rather than volume dictating the choice of drawbar outfit. BOC needed good manoevrability and compact overall dimensions, resulting in this 22 ton gtw self-loading lorry with matching York drawbar trailer for carrying palletised gas cylinders.
*(Vauxhall Motors Ltd)*

Heatons Transport of St. Helens operated a distribution contract with Matthews Office Furniture for which they used a fleet of drawbar outfits including this 1981 Bedford TL 1260 which went on the road in the first production year of the new TL range. It featured a swap body system by A.C. Penman. *(Vauxhall Motors Ltd)*

The need for maximum productivity and quick turn round led Whitbread to experiment with this special KME 6x2 low loading outfit hauling a single axle 'Urban artic' semi trailer coupled to a fifth wheel dolly. On arrival at its destination the drawing vehicle could carry on solo for pub deliveries while a Bedford TK 'Urban' tractor was employed to take the semi trailer on another delivery round. After the deliveries were completed the 6x2 was once again hitched to the semi trailer for the long distance journey back to the brewery. *(A. Ingram)*

Launched in 1974 the Bedford TM heavyweight range included numerous four and six wheeled models for drawbar use. This lefthand drive Detroit Diesel powered 'EWV3' was put into operation as a promotional demonstrator unit for UK and European dealer shows. It features a York drawbar trailer and carries two matching 24ft York van bodies. Power unit was the 222 bhp V6 2-stroke Detroit Diesel with Fuller RTO 609 transmission. *(Vauxhall Motors Ltd)*

An alternative power unit, the 150 bhp '500-151' in-line six 4-stroke diesel, later replaced by the '8.2 Blue Series', was available for TMs. This EMV3, one of the first to enter service was used by a large Kent farming operation to deliver produce to wholesale markets and supermarket chains. *(Vauxhall Motors Ltd)*

# BRISTOL

1953 Bristol HG6L drawbar outfit. Based at Birmingham, this was one of a large fleet operated by British Road Services during the Fifties. Powered by the Leyland O.600 oil engine, the HG6L was designed exclusively for BRS as their standard maximum-capacity long distance vehicle. 517 were built with a variety of cabs, this example having a Burlingham. Relatively few of them were operated with drawbar trailers. *(Author)*

# COMMER

This 1937 'LN5' is seen coupled to a Tasker 4-ton drawbar trailer. It was one of two similar vehicles operated by fruit and vegetable growers L J Knight Ltd of Ringwood, Hants. Standard power unit for the LN5 was the 80 bhp 4.1 litre 6-cylinder side valve petrol. The Perkins Leopard II diesel was optional for an extra £200 — a considerable premium in view of the £319 price tag for the complete petrol-engined model. *(W. Packham)*

Vehicles like this 1951 Commer QX with 109 bhp semi horizontal petrol engine would not have been a common choice for drawbar operation. Perhaps it was intended for hauling light ale! Actually the real payload limit would be in the region of 10-12 tons.
*(A. Ingram collection)*

*(Below):* Eight Hillman Minx body shells form a relatively light cargo for this 1958 Rootes TS3 diesel-powered Commer drawbar transporter operated by BRS Oxford Branch who ran a specialised service for the motor industry.
*(A. Ingram)*

*(Above):* DAF 2500 close coupled outfit in service with Carman Transport's subsidiary, Brit-European. Miles-Nunn bodywork and trailer provide 130 cu.m. of load volume, the roof of the curtainsider body being adjustable for height. A special extendable drawbar is fitted for negotiating tight turns. The outfit is employed on the delivery of JCB diggers to European customers. *(J. Taylor)*

1986 DAF 2100 drawbar outfit with swap body system. It is one of a number in service with United Carriers and their associate, Sovereign, on UK parcels service. *(Author)*

*(Right):* This DAF F2200 hauled outfit dates from 1974 when it was operated by the well known Scottish Inveresk Paper Co Ltd. DAF's UK marketing drive was under way in the early 70s bringing continental standards of comfort and power to the British operator. The F2200 grossed up to 19 tons solo and 32 tons train weight and was powered by the relatively small DU825 8.25 litre turbo diesel developing 218 bhp. *(Author)*

*(Below right):* Leyland-DAF 2100 drawbar model featuring the 228 bhp version of the 8.25 turbo. This outfit has close coupled centre-bogie trailer with high volume curtainsider bodywork. Extra body length comes from the use of a day cab with a cab top sleeper pod. It is one of a fleet operated by Westermann UK. *(Author)*

*(Top far right):* While Dennis Bros. history goes back to the very dawn of motoring, few records exist of Dennis drawbar outfits, certainly in the post war period. This rather unusual lightweight outfit from the mid 30s, with typical extravagant body styling was operated by Portsmouth-based Chapmans Laundry. It might never have been photographed had it not taken part in this carnival parade. *(W. Packham)*

*(Bottom far right):* Dodge were not so common as drawbars but Osram-GEC Lighting operated this smart outfit hauled by a 1973 tilt-cab K900. The York van trailer is composed of a lightweight step-frame semi trailer with a single axle on small diameter wheels coupled to a fifth wheel dolly with standard 20in wheels. *(Author)*

# DENNIS

# DODGE

The varied fleet of Union Cartage Company 'tugs' used around the London Dock area included this unusual Dodge D309 Series with a composite cab, the doors and back panel of which are of the standard 'LAD' type. It was captured on camera in the Silvertown area hauling a 16ft drawbar trailer with lift-off insulated container. *(Author)*

Dating from 1981 this Perkins-engined Dodge 100 series outfit from the fleet of Silentnight Bedding of Barnoldswick, Lancashire, carries two identical demountable van bodies. Low profile tyres are fitted to the truck to achieve minimum loading height.
*(M. Cramp)*

Latest development of the Dodge marque within the Renault Vehicules Industriels empire was this 100 Series seen here with high volume van bodywork, part of the Walkers of Wakefield fleet.
*(Author)*

ERF

*(Top far left):* ERF were a relatively new make when this CI.5 was built in 1936 having only begun production in 1933. It is as near a perfect example of the traditional old style British trailer outfit as you could find. The make of trailer is uncertain but it has many of the characteristics of the Carrimore. The outfit was part of the well known W.H. Bowker fleet from Blackburn. *(A. Ingram)*

*(Bottom far left):* As this photograph shows, ERF had hardly changed in appearance during their first six years of production. This machine bears a 1939 registration number and was operated in conjunction with its Dyson drawbar trailer by Dee Valley Transport of Llangollen. *(E. Wyles)*

*(Top left):* 1952 ERF 6.6 with 18ft Tasker trailer photographed in Liverpool Docks. The lorry features ERF's new look V-front cab often referred to as the Jennings Streamline. The outfit was operated by Reliance Motors of Bolton in the 60s. *(Author)*

*(Left):* These ballasted drawbar tractors hauling heavy independent trailers were common around the dock areas. Bibby's at Liverpool ran a number of them including this 1947 example, the cab of which is a V-front type similar to the Reliance vehicle but featuring the older 'exposed' radiator. The trailer grossed about 18 tons, having twin oscillating rear axles. *(Author)*

*(Above):* An exceptionally long 'train' of three living vans is seen behind this purpose-built showman's unit delivered new to Botton Bros. of Farnborough, Kent, in 1946. It is an ERF CI.6. *(ERF Ltd)*

Burton Transport, the transport subsidiary of brewers, Ind Coope and Allsop, operated this nicely liveried ERF 6.6 outfit with drawbar trailer which appears to be a Taskers. *(A. Ingram)*

A late version of the 'KV' cab adorns this Gardner 6LX-powered Chinese Six and trailer operated by Scott's of Oldham, much of whose work was for United Glass. It is pictured at Scott's own depot in Barton Street, Oldham.
(R. Kenney)

(Below): Ultimate development of Britain's classic eight wheeler and trailer, represented here by a 1963 ERF 6.8GX with the early 'LV' cab. This class of outfit was killed off by legislative changes in the mid Sixties. It is powered by a Gardner '150' 6LX and is an excellent example of a lost breed.
(R. Kenney)

*(Above):* Though four years later than the Knowles' outfit (pages 42/43) this 1977 ERF of Bonar Bibby & Baron harks back to the old style outfit, having single wheels all round on the trailer.
*(Author)*

A comfortable night's sleep should be no problem with this high-cube close-coupled outfit hauled by a 1984 M-series. A generous cab top 'pod' has been neatly fared in to match the height of the demountable box body. The centre bogie type trailer carries a matching box.
*(Author)*

Though beginning to show its age this 32-ton gtw combination has been included as an example of utilising a standard semi trailer and fifth wheel dolly to form a drawbar trailer. It consists of an ERF LAC320 coupled to a tandem axle York Freightmaster van. *(Author)*

*(Below):* Following the trends of the 90s, this Cummins-powered E8 outfit of Ansell's Brewery has all the latest features. The centre bogie 'drawbar semi', once confined to certain European countries, shows signs of ousting the traditional British two-axle drawbar trailer. *(Author)*

After the requirement for a statutory attendant was dropped in 1970 drawbar outfits became more profitable to operate. By that time multi-wheelers offered no train weight advantage so the most popular combination was the high-powered four wheeler at 32 tons gross, like this Cummins-powered ERF which was new to Knowles Transport of Wimblington in 1972. (A. Knowles)

FODEN

*(Top far left):* Recalling the steam era is this 1923 C-type 6-ton overtype in the livery of flour millers A. & A. Peate from Oswestry. Just behind it is the Foden-built drawbar trailer with which it operated. Being on solid tyres it was limited to 12 mph maximum speed. *(Author's collection)*

*(Top left):* This dockland scene in Liverpool shows one of the typical ballast tractor and drawbar configurations seen in that area. The heavy trailer with twin oscillating rear axles carries a load of Guinness Export tanks and is hauled by a 1947 Foden DG from Jarvis Robinson Transport, Bootle. *(Author)*

*(Middle left):* Not many hauliers chose Foden eight wheelers for trailer work but this impressive outfit is hauled by a 1955 FG6/15. It belonged to Eye Haulage from Suffolk and is seen fully loaded with bagged potatoes. Later in life the vehicle spent some years with Tommy Wilson's Funfair before being acquired by John Pearson for preservation, though the drawbar trailer has long since vanished. The Foden had a 112 bhp Gardner 6LW oil engine. *(G Lock)*

*(Left):* Another of the few firms to run Foden eight wheelers and trailers was The Motor Packing Co Ltd from Coventry. This FE6/15 was photographed laden with timber in Liverpool Docks in the mid Sixties. *(Author)*

Many old lorries survive in showland service for years after retirement from regular haulage. This early post war Foden DG6/15 was 20 years old when photographed but was still in remarkably good order. A bold rooftop sign (with spelling mistake!) warns oncoming motorists of the outfit's overall length which includes a low-bed drawbar trailer. *(Author)*

*(Below):* Bulky plastic foam requires maximum cubic capacity — achieved by Harrison & Jones' maximum length drawbar outfits. Foden four wheelers are uncommon but this shot captures a convoy of three at once, heading home up the M1 motorway. *(Author)*

Toleman's Car Delivery Service operated this Ford D2817 from Dagenham on the delivery of Ford cars. It was one of ten such combinations powered by the '511' V8 diesel and designed for 28 tons gtw. Bodywork and trailer were by Anthony Carrimore. *(Ford Motor Co)*

*(Below):* Early Seventies York Skipmaster outfit employs a trailer similar to that of the latest close-coupled high-cube trailer combination. It is hauled by a Ford D series. *(York Trailer Co)*

*(Above):* 1975 saw the launch of Ford's new Transcontinental range for up to 42 tons gtw. This Crane Fruehauf bodied 6x4-hauled outfit to TIR specification is one of Ford's own demonstration units. Under UK weight laws drawbar outfits are limited to 32 tons. *(Ford Motor Co)*

Dairy Products Transport, formerly the Milk Marketing Board, operate a number of these specialised bulk milk farm collection tankers based on Ford Cargos. This one is seen waiting to unload at Longley Farm Dairies of Holmfirth in the Pennines. *(J. Taylor)*

It might be stretching a point to include this Thames ET6 mobile bookshop but at least it shows a commercial application at the lighter end of the weight range. *(Author)*

*(Below):* A rare example of the short-lived Fowler diesel. This 1931 90 bhp 'Marathon' was of heavy specification, specially aimed at trailer operation but owing to its high cost and heavy construction could not compete successfully with such makes as AEC and Leyland from the same period. It was built in Leeds by John Fowler & Co, a name chiefly associated with steam vehicles. *(A. Ingram collection)*

# FOWLER

*(Top far left):* London Carriers, who handled the distribution of electrical goods, ran a number of large capacity Guy Big J trailer outfits of which this is a typical example. It was new in 1972 and features a York single axle semi trailer and fifth wheel dolly. *(Author)*

*(Top left):* Guy were latecomers to the eight wheeler business beginning in 1954 with their AEC-based Invincible Mk.I. In 1958 the completely new Mk.II range was introduced. Most common power unit was the Gardner 150 but optional engines including Leyland were available. In spite of its ample choice of power ratings and heavily specified running units, not many were seen on drawbar work. This one was engaged on general haulage with East London based F. Jones & Sons. *(Author)*

*(Left):* This well matched outfit dating from around 1970 comprises a Guy Big J4 and York drawbar trailer equipped with matching Boalloy Tautliner body for the Automotive Products Group of Leamington Spa. *(Author's collection)*

LEYLAND

*(Top, far left):* Leylands have always been popular for trailer operation. This early Twenties shot shows a solid-tyred RAF type with lift-off container in use by the famous Pickfords Removals company at their Truro branch in Cornwall. *(Author's collection)*

*(Bottom, far left):* This scene, rich in atmosphere, depicts an early Thirties Beaver and trailer from the W.H. Bowker fleet, one of the largest and best known haulage companies in the North West. *(W.H. Bowker)*

*(Top left):* Vividly recalling the wartime era when the 'blackout' required lorries to have headlamp masks and white edged mudguards, this photograph shows a true long distance drawbar outfit of the period. It is a 1937 Leyland Hippo, also part of the large W.H. Bowker fleet from Blackburn. *(W.H. Bowker)*

*(Left):* This 1934 Beaver, part of the Hovis fleet, features an unusual cab design peculiar to that operator. The distinctive headboard and deep body sides provided extra advertising space. This example, fleet number 126, was photographed in London when 16 years old. *(A. Ingram)*

A fine twin steer Beaver of 1937 vintage in the livery of Cronton Haulage Co Ltd of Cronton, near Widnes. Seen from this high vantage point, the difference in lock angles of the two front steering axles is clear, the first axle lock being greater than the second to achieve correct tracking. This model later became the 'Steer' and was popular for trailer use in spite of its heavy steering and short rear overhang which made reversing trickier. (*J. Richardson collection*)

1946 12.1B 'Interim' Beaver gallantly working on in the mid Sixties. The model, powered by Leyland's 7.4 litre diesel engine, was only in production for approximately 12 months. This was one of a number operated by Shorts of Halifax on wool traffic.
*(Author)*

An example of the 12.B/1 Beaver dating from 1948. It was operated by Barton's Cooperage for the transport of empty casks. The tall cage style Luton body was by Bonallack & Sons and is a good example of a drawbar outfit providing extra load volume as opposed to weight. Note the small 13in wheels on the trailer to gain maximum load height. By contrast the lorry is shod on '40x8s'.
*(Bonallack/A. Hustwitt)*

Harrison's of Dewsbury were one of the best known companies operating a regular Yorkshire to London trunk service during the Fifties and Sixties. Here a 1956 Steer 'Chinese Six' and drawbar trailer is seen parked up in London awaiting the nightman to begin the return journey to Dewsbury, near Leeds. The Luton type van body and the trailer both have open roofs for overhead loading, the load being protected by tarpaulin sheets. *(A. Ingram)*

Descendant of the BMC this 1971 Perkins engined Mastiff bears a Leyland name badge, being part of the Red Line range. From the mid Sixties onwards the traditional lightweight mass produced trucks such as BMC, Bedford and Ford, began to move up the weight range to compete with the established British 'heavies'. *(Author)*

(Above): The Leyland Marathon owes its parentage to AEC Ltd and while long wheelbase models were available they were far less common than tractor units. Drawbar outfits like this rare example sometimes started life as tractor units only to be converted into long wheelbase trucks later on for drawbar use. (Author)

Another striking example of a Marathon in use as a trailer outfit. This one has had a sleeper extension added plus a self-loading crane for handling round timber. (Author)

*(Above):* In Britain tank bodied drawbar outfits are quite unusual but in recent years there has been an increase of the type on milk transport. This outfit from the fleet of G. Easton Ltd is based on a 1986 Cruiser. *(J. Taylor)*

The 'Power Plus' Octopus was an ideal machine for trailer work having a choice of power ratings up to 200 bhp. This smart outfit featuring the all-steel LAD cab was one of a number of eight wheelers and trailers from the Barrow in Furness fleet of Athersmith Bros. *(Author)*

Possibly the most popular lorry of its era for drawbar use, the Octopus saw service in many major fleets throughout the UK. Among the last operators to use them were G.A. Day Ltd, the builders merchants from Portsmouth, Hants. This 1960 air-braked 24.O/4 from the last year of production before the launch of the Power-Plus range, was one of three in the Day fleet still working in the early Seventies.
*(Author)*

*(Top far left):* MAN is one of the European makes that started to win popularity in the UK during the mid Seventies. Its native Germany is true drawbar territory and this 1981 '16.280' outfit, though photographed in the north of England, bears a distinct Continental air, heightened by the single tyred tag axle and TIR tilt bodywork. *(J. Taylor)*

*(Bottom, far left):* A short cab is featured on this 19.321 high volume close-coupled outfit, one of a number operated by Carmans Brit-European. The cab top sleeper helps to achieve maximum body length. The effect of uneven ground on close-coupled outfits is seen here where there is sometimes a risk of lorry and trailer 'fouling' at roof level — a problem overcome by automatically extending drawbars. *(Author)*

*(Top left):* A most impressive outfit is this 1986 19.361 coupled to a 3-axle curtainsider trailer. The lorry has a skeletal body with 6m ISO container and advertises the operator's 24 hour Manchester to Paris service. *(J. Taylor)*

*(Left):* Clean lines characterise this 1990 MAN 17.232FD 'F90' model with sleeper cab in the silver livery of UGI Meters Ltd from London. In drawbar form the 17.232 is powered by MAN's 6.87 litre six cylinder turbo diesel rated at 230bhp. *(Author)*

MAUDSLAY

*(Top far left):* Small headlamps and a mesh grille plus an in-cab radiator filler date this Maudslay Mogul Mk.1 as being a late wartime model from about 1945. Standard power unit for the Mogul was the AEC 7.7 litre oil engine. This smart outfit with Dyson trailer came from the well known H.L. Walker fleet from Thornaby on Tees which was absorbed into Smith of Maddiston during the Sixties.
*(Author s collection)*

*(Bottom, far left):* By 1949 Maudslays had been given a smart new cast aluminium radiator. Such features were restricted during the war years when the metal was scarce and in great demand by the aircraft industry. This is a Mogul Mk.3 and trailer in the livery of the large London haulage company C. Grace & Sons and is loaded with bagged CWS flour.
*(A. Ingram)*

*(Top left):* Best remembered heroes of the haulage world were the long distance heavies like this 1949 BRS Parcels Maudslay Meritor outfit which was engaged on the regular London South Yorkshire trunk. Meritors were powered by the AEC 9.6 litre oil engine and had a David Brown 557 gearbox. The majority of those built went to BRS. This one features the Tillotson cab favoured by that operator.
*(A. Ingram)*

*(Left):* Sutton & Son (St. Helens) Ltd are best known for their impressive Atkinson fleet but they did operate a variety of other makes. This handsome Mustang is believed to have been the only Maudslay on their large fleet and is seen here heading out of London in the evening along the A1.
*(A. Ingram)*

The tractor unit offered by Maudslay in the immediate postwar years was known as the Maharanee and was similar to the Mogul but on a shorter wheelbase. Here a Maharanee ballast tractor in the smart brown and gold leaf livery of R. Cornell hauls a 10-ton insulated van trailer through the busy streets of London s East End.
*(A. Ingram)*

MERCEDES

*(Top far left):* A typical example of Mercedes drawbar outfits is this 17-20 from Hedley s Humpers of North Acton. Mercedes are perfectly suited to such work, coming from a country where trailer operation is widely favoured and outfits are permitted to run more competitively at 38 tonnes gross. *(Author)*

*(Top left):* Where light, bulky goods are concerned such as plastic containers, low weight and relatively low powered vehicles like this 13-ton gvw Mercedes 1317 are often chosen for drawbar work. This outfit from Plysu has large volume curtain sided swap bodies and features low profile tyres to reduce the vehicle height. The attractive cab is that introduced on the new lightweight 6.5 to 11 tonnes gvw range launched in 1984. *(Author)*

*(Left):* British makes have faced increasing competition from European manufacturers during the past two decades. In the Sixties it was very unusual to see anything other than British trucks but European machines like this Mercedes 1625 are now commonplace. *(J. Taylor)*

MORRIS COMMERCIAL

*(Top far left):* An example of a lightweight drawbar outfit from the Thirties. This Morris Commercial CS13/60F semi forward control 3-tonner has had its load capacity doubled by the addition of a trailer. In this case the load of empty crates is light but bulky so the lorry is not over stressed. *(A. Ingram collection)*

*(Bottom far left):* The Courier was Morris Commercial's pre war 'heavyweight' attempting to compete in the Leyland and AEC class. It is believed to be the only full forward control lorry on 10-stud wheels to have appeared from the company and is seen here in drawbar form wearing the livery of Trutime Deliveries of Newcastle on Tyne. Power unit was a 5.1 litre 4-cylinder petrol engine. *(A. Ingram collection)*

*(Top left):* When it comes to rare drawbar outfits this one takes some beating. The Morris Commercial FV was not really designed for such work but the owner of this Channel Islands outfit was getting full value for money by coupling up to a Dyson 8-ton drawbar trailer which would be more at home behind a Leyland Octopus. *(A. Ingram)*

*(Left):* The same Channel Islands operator, J. & D. Norman Ltd of Guernsey, owned this later FFK100 powered by the 90 bhp 5.1 litre 6-cylinder BMC diesel. Designed for a nominal payload of 5 tons the FFK100 was not often seen in drawbar form. *(A. Ingram)*

RENAULT

SCAMMELL

*(Top far left):* What was once the Commer plant in Dunstable and later Chrysler, who manufactured Dodge trucks, became part of Renault Vehicles Industriels in the early 80s. Subsequently UK-assembled Renaults such as this G170 became more common. This outfit with alloy dropside bodywork is operated by Northamptonshire-based Potters Haulage. *(Author)*

*(Bottom far left):* Less common in drawbar form is this R310, with a design gvw of 19 tons, which Renault developed from the old Berliet range. Powered by the 305 bhp MIDR.06 35 40 6-cylinder turbo diesel, this outfit from R.W. Feather of Bradford has a curtainsider body while the trailer, which apparently pre-dates the sideguard regulations, has a TIR tilt. *(Author)*

*(Top left):* Scammell became famous for their Articulated Six Wheelers from the early 1920s and are seldom thought of as producers of orthodox 4-wheeled lorries. However, this photograph dating from the early 30s depicts an impressive long wheelbase bonneted dropside coupled to a Scammell 4-wheel drawbar trailer. The trailer features Ackerman type steering eliminating the 'fifth wheel' turntable and permitting a lower body height. *(Author's collection)*

*(Left):* In 1962 came the Routeman II with its ultra modern styling by Michelloti. Routeman models had a choice of Leyland or Gardner power, Scammell's having become part of the Leyland Group in 1955. This 1964 Routeman II with a typical period 16ft 8-ton trailer is in the livery of the Hull Fish Meal & Oil Co and was photographed on the Welwyn Bypass. *(Author)*

*(Above):* A well matched Scammell Rigid Eight and trailer with wooden dropside bodywork. This 1950 giant for a Staffordshire haulier was powered by the 102 bhp Gardner 6LW and featured Scammell's own design of 6-speed gate-change gearbox and single drive, double reduction rear bogie. Despite its massive proportions this outfit was remarkably light, weighing under 9 tons unladen.
*(Author's collection)*

Featuring Leyland's High Datum sleeper cab as fitted to the Roadtrain, this 1985 S26 with Rolls Royce 265 Turbo diesel power represents the latter day products from Scammell. By this time it had become Leyland's Special Purpose and Military Vehicle Division and civilian haulage examples like this one were few and far between. With a design gross train weight of 38 tons, the outfit is limited by UK legislation to 32 tons.
*(J. Taylor)*

Coming from a country where goods transport is dominated by drawbar outfits, Scanias are well suited to UK trailer work. While Swedish drawbar outfits can gross up to 52 tonnes at their maximum 24m length limit, British versions are more modest as UK legislation limits them to 32 tons and 18.35m. J.T. Padbury of Northampton ran this 1974 '80' model on livestock haulage. *(Author)*

*(Below):* While most UK operators favour artics for general haulage, drawbar outfits are sometimes preferred especially where extra load volume is required. Also, remarkably, an outfit of this type could be driven on a 'class 3' HGV licence, the test for which was less demanding than a 'class 1'. Looking very much a typical haulage lorry with its old style sheeted load, this 1981 registered '82M' is in the livery of Michael R. Spurr from Ossett in West Yorkshire. *(J. Taylor)*

Drawbar tankers are relatively uncommon in Britain but collection and delivery of fresh milk is one type of traffic in which they have gained popularity, especially in the Pennine area. Typical is this 1987 '92M' of S.J. Bargh of Caton near Lancaster, seen delivering to Longley Farm Dairies near Holmfirth. (*J. Taylor*)

Though hauled by a Swedish-sourced truck, this outfit has a strong British character. The 93H like most Swedish six wheelers is a 6x2. This one is operated by Roy Butt of Doddscombsleigh, Exeter who has made good use of the statutory sideguards to advertise his services to Cornwall, Midlands and the North. The vehicle was photographed at Charnock Richard in Lancs.
*(Author)*

# SEDDON

Drawbar combinations come into their own on parcels work where extra load volume is the main requirement. This 1974 Seddon 16 Four DB is a nicely matched van outfit from the Hinckley based fleet of Bees Transport. It is powered by a Gardner '6LXB' 180 with which it grossed 30 tons gtw. (Seddon Atkinson)

(Bottom far left): Many hauliers of the Forties and Fifties were quite happy to lump 10 tons or more on to a 6/7 tonner but this 1944 Seddon Mk 5L of Dukes of Bishops Waltham shares its burden with a small drawbar trailer. With a train weight in the region of 15-16 tons the Perkins P6 would have had to work quite hard on hills. (Perkins Engines)

(Left): Demountable 'swap' bodies can extend the versatility of drawbar outfits even further by cutting down on waiting time for loading and unloading. This 1975 Seddon 16-Four DB has a demountable box van and pulls a heavy duty van trailer, the combined outfit measuring approximately 18m in length. Usual power unit was the Rolls Royce Eagle 270. The lower cost 205 bhp Perkins V8 was also offered in these purpose-built trailer models. (Author)

SEDDON ATKINSON

*(Top far left):* Countrywide Eggs of Leominster operated this 1976 sleeper-cabbed 400 Series to distribute their produce. Powered by an 8LXB Gardner '240' it has a demountable insulated van body. Note the specially fitted front towing jaw for shunting. *(Author)*

*(Bottom far left):* Introduced in 1983 the 401 Series had a facelifted cab based on the 400 design. This smart 32-ton outfit in the livery of Goldwells of East Malling has a Rolls Royce 265L and a curtainsider body but pulls a flat platform trailer. *(Author)*

*(Top left):* Motoring steadily up the A74 near the Scottish border, this 1981 outfit resembles a 401 Series but is, in fact, a 400. Many old 400s were updated with smart new 40l grilles. This general haulage outfit in the livery of RDB Freight Lines, Sheffield, hauls a fifth wheel dolly and single axle semi trailer. *(Author)*

*(Left):* For lighter duties the Seddon Atkinson 200 was sometimes equipped for trailer use. This one, in the Shepton Mallet based fleet of Showerings Ltd, hauls a trailer which has 16in wheels and a pair of matching demountable box bodies. The 200 Series models were powered by the 134 bhp International Harvester D358 Diesel. *(J. Taylor)*

After the merger of
Atkinson and Seddon in
1970 the first Seddon
Atkinson 400 Series
appeared in 1975. This
picture shows an early
example of a maximum
capacity drawbar outfit
in the livery of well
known Scottish haulier
MacBraynes.
*(Seddon Atkinson)*

SENTINEL

*(Top far left):* This 1931 Sentinel DG4 chain drive steamer from the fleet of Paul Bros, pulls a Dyson trailer adding about 60% more payload capacity. Long before bulk handling and palletisation, bagged flour was hand loaded from overhead shutes or conveyors. The rear loading board on the trailer was preferred for this type of operation and continued to be seen until the early Sixties. *(Author's collection)*

*(Bottom far left):* Sentinel's S type range included this S4 dating from 1933 operated by Rainford Potteries. An outfit such as this was allowed to run at 24 tons gross, 2 tons more than a petrol lorry as steamers had to carry the extra weight of coal and water. Taxation by unladen weight from the early Thirties helped to force steamers off the roads. *(A. Ingram collection)*

*(Top left):* Fletcher's of Ibstock, Leicestershire, were one of the best known users of Sentinel lorries and were part of a group specialising in coal haulage. This 'DV66M' with Sentinel's 9.1 litre 6-cylinder underfloor engine, hauled a tipping trailer, the outfit grossing 32 tons. The vehicle was later converted into a rigid eight wheeler by TVW at Warrington. *(Author's collection)*

*(Left):* A DV64 Sentinel hides behind its Dyson 8-ton trailer in an East London haulage yard in the early 60s. Following the end of Sentinel's diesel production in 1956 these well engineered machines soon disappeared. The suspicious owner of this one denied access to the photographer. *(Author)*

THORNYCROFT

*(Top far left):* A particularly well proportioned outfit is this mid Thirties 'Trusty' belonging to Thomas Allen and operated on the Park Royal Transport fleet distributing Guinness products. A set back front axle with low cab entry steps are features associated with more modern post war designs. *(Author's collection)*

*(Top left):* With only 100 bhp and 320 lb.ft of torque from its 7.9 litre 6-cylinder oil engine, the Thornycroft PF.NR6/MV eight wheeler was not the first choice for drawbar operation. By comparison AEC's 9.6 litre-powered rival produced 125 bhp and 430 lb.ft. Not surprisingly there are few photographs of Thornycroft eight wheelers and trailers so this one from the fleet of Mortons is something of a rarity. The trailer with its small wheels appears to be of lightweight specification. *(Author's collection)*

*(Left):* Dating from the 1934 period this impressive line-up shows four bonneted Thornycrofts, apparently Taurus models, in the process of being loaded at Barclay Perkins & Co Ltd of London. The set back front axle not only improved weight distribution and engine access but aided manoeuvrability. Note the 'Danger' sign hanging from the trailer drawbar. *(Author's collection)*

VOLVO

*(Top far left):* The late Sixties marked the arrival in Britain of significant numbers of imported European trucks. Among the most successful of these was the Volvo F86. This nicely matched combination of a 16-ton gross tipper and tipping trailer was an early example to enter the fleet of Kingscliffe Super Refractories in Sheffield. *(Author's collection)*

*(Bottom far left):* From the late sixties, trials were carried out to assess the use of 'double-bottom' outfits in the UK. This Swedish style combination hauled by an F86 tractor unit was well over the UK 18m length limit but some trials were conducted at a military test track in Surrey. *(Author's collection)*

*(Top left):* After tests were conducted between 1967 and 1972 a 'double-bottom' measuring 18m was allowed to run on feasibility trials in 1976. Some operators including Reed Transport, Whitworths Foods and H.H. Robertson of Ellesmere Port, were given special permission by the Department of Transport to assess the outfits for a limited period. This G89 hauled 'doubles' outfit appeared at the 1973 Lorry Driver of the Year Finals at Bramcote. *(Author)*

*(Left):* In spite of its seven axles, giving a potential capacity of about 60 tons, this striking outfit consisting of an F7 six wheeled tipper with single axle dolly and triaxle bulk semi can only gross 32 tons under UK legislation. *(J Taylor)*

One time users of AEC vehicles, the London Brick Co added large numbers of Volvos to their ranks from the late Sixties onwards. Predominantly F86 six wheelers and artics, the fleet also included this somewhat rarer type consisting of an FB88 and drawbar trailer, based at Stewartby Works near Bedford. (Author)

*(Above):* A more typically British outfit is this well laden F7 of Charles Footman from Carmarthen in Dyfed, South Wales. This is a good instance where maximum load volume is required for bulky goods like straw bales. *(Author)*

Reminiscent of Swedish style outfits this F12 6x2 of P.D. Taylor from Brownhills, Staffordshire, has a day cab for maximum body length. A left hand drive machine, it was specially imported by the operator and features matching TIR tilt bodywork on the lorry and trailer. *(Author)*

The lighter 15-ton gvw FL6 introduced in 1986. Though powered by the small 204 bhp 5.48 litre engine, it can gross up to 20 tons with trailer. This Hovis outfit makes an interesting comparison with the Leyland Beaver from that company illustrated on p.53. (Author)

(Below): W.H. Bowker have always kept pace with the latest trends. Bowker International Transport, as they are now known, were among the first to operate a fleet of maximum cube close-coupled outfits similar to this F10 employed on regular Continental traffic. (Author)

This FL6, one of two such outfits operated by Guyhirn-based Ken Thomas Ltd, carries polystyrene blocks used in insulation. The total payload weighs only 4 tons. Standard gtw is 15.5 tons but this has been specially uprated to provide for additional ballast in the form of three water-filled tanks (utilising Volvo fuel tanks) on the lorry to make the outfit stable in cross winds. The trailer is of heavy construction to also aid stability, itself weighing 5 tons unladen.
*(Author)*

*(Below):* Vulcan, who ceased product on in 1952, were not often used for drawbar work. This 1944 model belonging to L.J. Knight Ltd of Ringwood, Hants is loaded with a wartime delivery of vegetables for the NAAFI. At 20 mph maximum there was no need to even rope the load. Note the headlamp masks and white edges to the mudguards — reminders of the 'blackout' era.
*(W Packham)*

# VULCAN

# DRAWBAR TRAILERS

## TRAILER MANUFACTURERS

Currently there are numerous UK companies who build drawbar trailers with or without bodywork to special order but, historically, the best known manufacturers are those listed below:

**'BTC' - British Trailer Co, Trafford Park**

**Boden Trailers Ltd, Oldham**

**J Brockhouse & Co Ltd, West Bromwich**

**Carrimore Six Wheelers Ltd, North Finchley**

**Cranes (Dereham) Ltd/Crane Fruehauf Trailers Ltd, Dereham**

**R A Dyson & Co Ltd, Liverpool**

**Eagle Engineering Co Ltd, Warwick**

**Hands (Letchworth) Ltd, Letchworth**

**Taskers of Andover (1932) Ltd, Andover**

**York Trailer Co, Corby**

Scammell Lorries' heavy duty Ackerman-steered trailer of the early Thirties

A heavy duty BTC drawbar trailer from the Forties.

Scammell's unusual Ackerman steering arrangement.

A medium weight drawbar trailer by Eagle Engineering from the Fifties.

Late Sixties Dyson heavy duty drawbar trailer.

*Trailer Manufacturers continued*

Taskers 8-ton van trailer for BRS Parcels, 1959.

Early Seventies low loading Dyson semi-trailer and fifth wheel dolly for brewery use.

Early Seventies Taskers F8 platform skeletal semi trailer coupled to an FO 9-ton fifth wheel dolly to form a full drawbar trailer.

Typical Dyson low loader type drawbar trailer with winch.

Taskers FO 9-ton fifth wheel dolly.

Dyson independent frame trailer for heavy indivisible loads.